Adventures in Ink

Be Mindful Be Calm

Daisy Seal

Uplifting, Calming Words · Perforated Pages for Framing
Over 100 Delightful Patterns

This is a **FLAME TREE** book | First published 2016

Publisher and Creative Director: Nick Wells
Senior Project Editor: Laura Bulbeck
Digital Manager: Chris Herbert
Art Director: Mike Spender

Special thanks to Frances Bodiam

Images in this book were crafted at the Flame Tree Studio, based on
illustrations © copyright Curly Pat, Tania Anisimova, anfisa focusova, Ryani
Kristina, ilonitta, Jake Jackson, Nairina, Plotnikova Olga, Rodina Olena,
Photo-Nuke, Saharinka, Tashsat, tets, Yoko Design.

© Flame Tree Publishing Ltd 2016

FLAME TREE PUBLISHING
6 Melbray Mews, Fulham,
London SW6 3NS, United Kingdom

www.flametreepublishing.com

ISBN: 978-1-80417-334-3

1 3 5 7 9 10 8 6 4 2
23 25 27 26 24

A CIP record for this book is available from the British Library upon request.

Printed in China | Created and designed in the UK

Adventures in Ink

Be Mindful
Be Calm
Daisy Seal

Uplifting, Calming Words · Perforated Pages for Framing
Over 100 Delightful Patterns

Words & Selection by Daisy Seal
Created by the Flame Tree Studio

FLAME TREE
PUBLISHING

My head, hot and fevered, rests upon the hills of my mind as I try to rest, and allow my thoughts to drift

From the buzz and drain of life. Patterns of the universe draw me upwards and I watch myself lift

Into the skies, watching my tense limbs from above, while I swim with clouds and play with butterflies,

Swirling in a circle around the world, teasing the dragons with laughter, and waiting for the moon to rise.

Adventures in Ink

Be Mindful
Be Calm

Such busy lives we lead! Sometimes we just need some relaxation and a little calm. This beautiful new book, created with a range of challenges, from easy and intermediate to the more detailed, will give you hours of calming entertainment. And now we've added a series of inspirational, mindful messages that weave through gently swirling backgrounds.

Be Mindful, Be Calm leads you through a series of reflections on life, our place in the universe, and our relationships with friends and family. The curl of vines, the flowing petals, and the symmetry of mandala patterns will provide that much needed rest from the chores and stresses of the day, helping us into a restful night's sleep.

As with the companion to this title, **Life Can Be Beautiful**, you can use a variety of pens: from gel and pencil, to pigment and crayon, from ballpoint and rollerball to highlighters, although it's best to avoid the heavy felt pens.

We designed the book so you can either colour the page with the hidden messages, or the image on the back, which is the same, but without the words. Each page is perforated near the spine of the book, so you can tear out and frame, perhaps even send them as a gift to a loved one.

Don't forget to sign your name at the bottom of the page, when you've finished each picture...

Beautifully inked by

Beautifully inked by

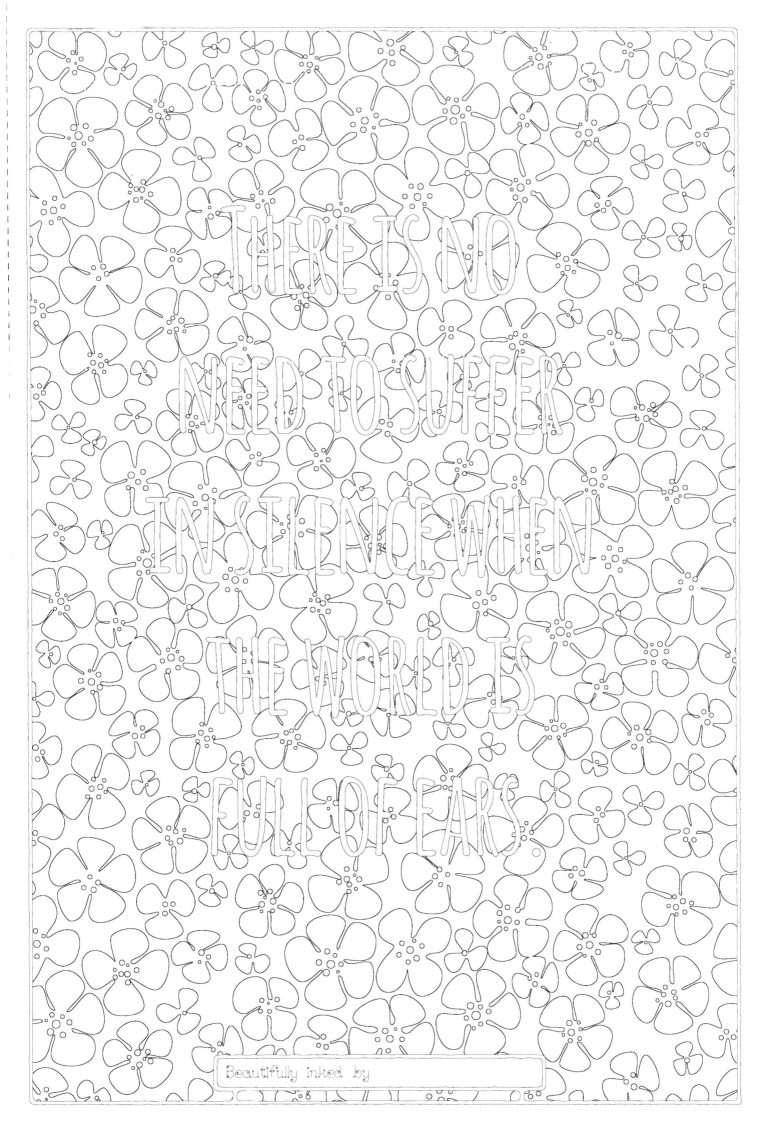

THERE IS NO NEED TO SUFFER IN SILENCE WHEN THE WORLD IS FULL OF EARS.

Beautifully inked by

Beautifully inked by

HOPE, LIKE THE TWILIGHT SUN, ALWAYS PROMISES TO RETURN.

Beautifully inked by

Beautifully inked by

WHEN THE SUN BREAKS THROUGH THE STORM, IT BREACHES THE TROUBLED MIND

Beautifully inked by

Beautifully inked by

Beautifully inked by

TAKE TIME

TO BE IN AWE

OF BEAUTY

Beautifully inked by

Beautifully inked by

Beautifully inked by

IN TIME, YOU WILL BALANCE THE FRENZY OF YOUR LIFE.

Beautifully inked by

Beautifully inked by

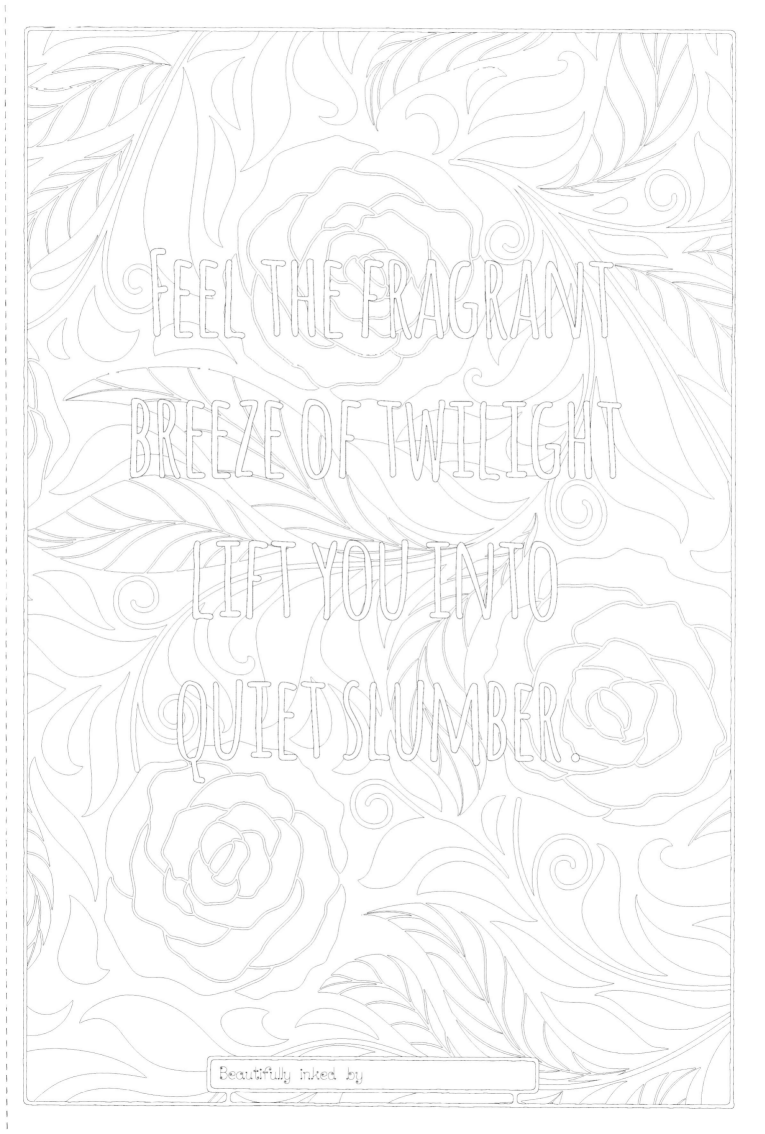

FEEL THE FRAGRANT BREEZE OF TWILIGHT LIFT YOU INTO QUIET SLUMBER.

Beautifully inked by

Beautifully inked by

ONCE YOU'VE FOUND YOUR WAY TO INNER CALM, NURTURE IT QUIETLY.

Beautifully inked by

Beautifully inked by

Beautifully inked by

CONFIDING IN A FRIEND CAN EASE YOUR INNER PAIN.

Beautifully inked by

Beautifully inked by

AS THE SUN RISES IT LIFTS AWAY THE UNCERTAINTIES OF NIGHT.

Beautifully inked by

Beautifully inked by

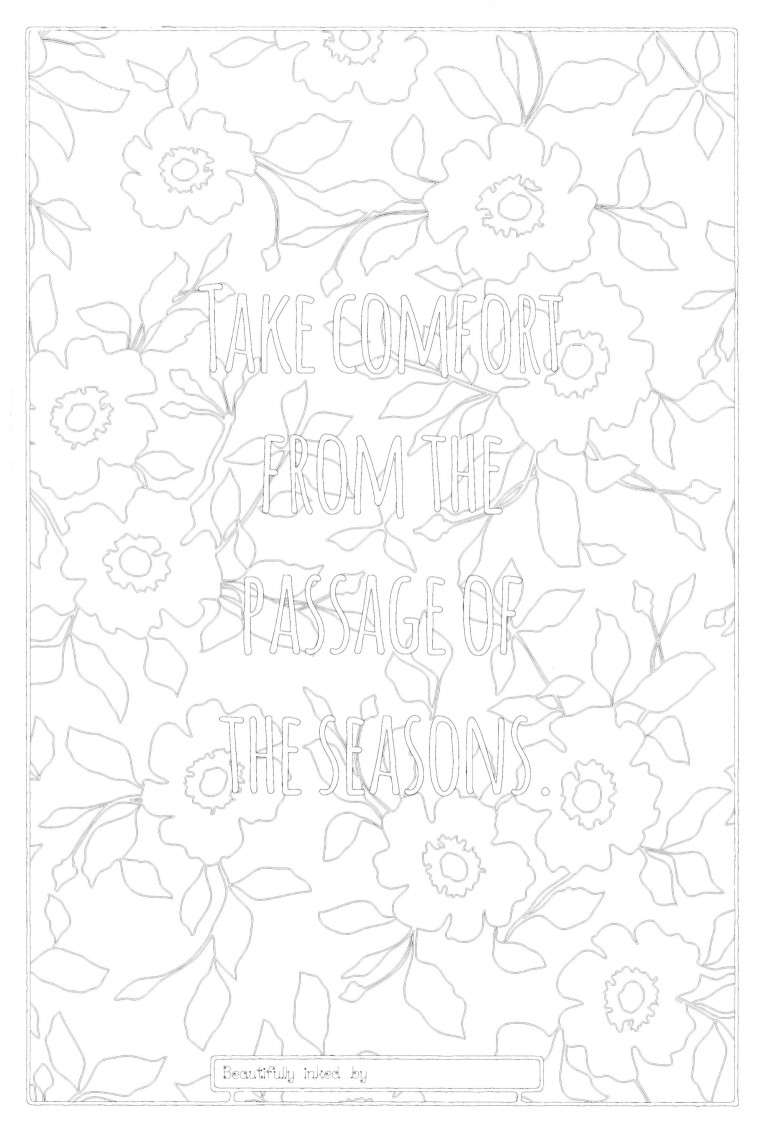

TAKE COMFORT
FROM THE
PASSAGE OF
THE SEASONS.

Beautifully inked by

Beautifully inked by

LET YOUR MIND SWIM WITH THE REFLECTIONS.

Beautifully inked by

Beautifully inked by

YOUR LIFE IS AN EVER-EXPANDING UNIVERSE. NEW EXPERIENCES EMERGE IN EVERY MOMENT.

Beautifully inked by

Beautifully inked by

Beautifully inked by

SWIM GENTLY THROUGH THE CALM POOLS OF MEMORY

Beautifully inked by

Beautifully inked by

Beautifully inked by

YOU WILL FIND COMFORT IN THE STILLNESS DEEP WITHIN YOU.

Beautifully inked by

Beautifully inked by

THE CHILD WITHIN YOU REMAINS, STILL, ALTHOUGH SHE SLEEPS INSIDE.

Beautifully inked by

Beautifully inked by

RAIN GLISTENS
ON YOUR FOREHEAD
TURNING SUPRISE
INTO QUIET JOY.

Beautifully inked by

Beautifully inked by

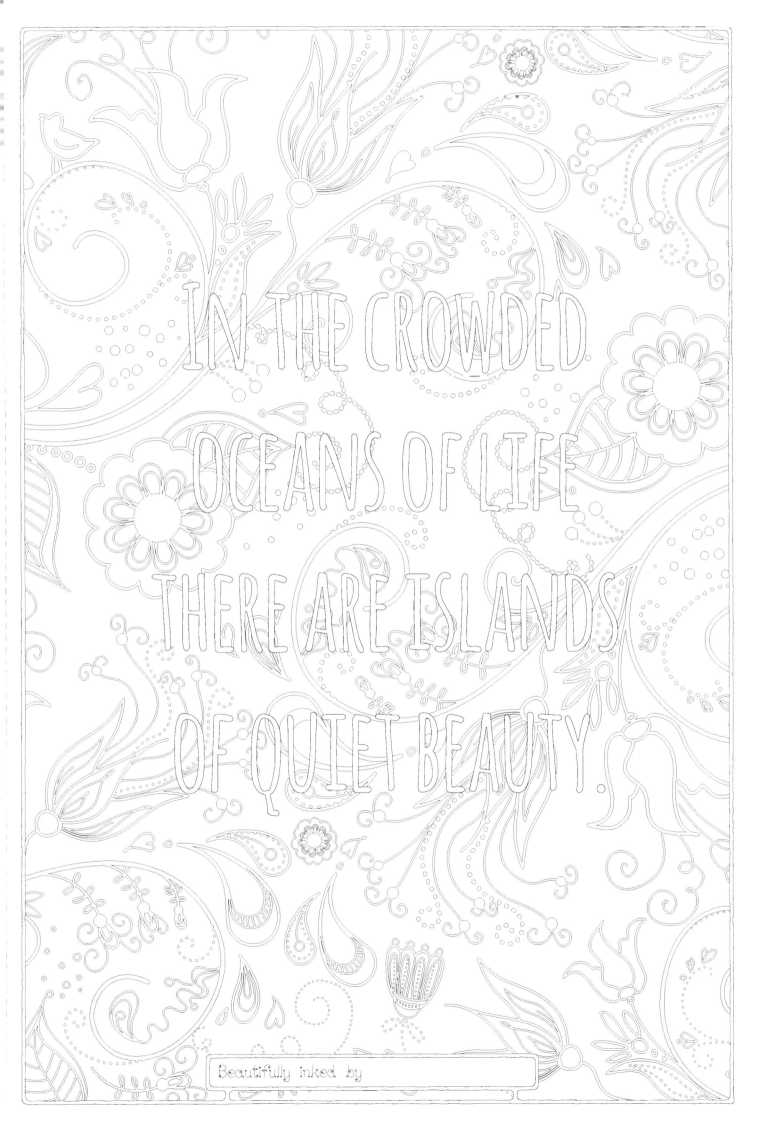

IN THE CROWDED OCEANS OF LIFE THERE ARE ISLANDS OF QUIET BEAUTY.

Beautifully inked by

Beautifully inked by

CALM YOUR BREATHING WITH THOUGHTS OF SUMMER BREEZES.

Beautifully inked by

Beautifully inked by

UNDERNEATH THE FRAUGHT SURFACE OF THE NOW, THERE IS A QUIET SHIVER OF THE FUTURE.

Beautifully inked by

Beautifully inked by

Beautifully inked by

THE SEARCH FOR
INNER BALANCE
ONLY REQUIRES
INNER BEAUTY.

Beautifully inked by

Beautifully inked by

THERE ARE MANY STEPS TO RECOVERY, BUT TAKEN ONE AT A TIME, YOU'LL HARDLY NOTICE THE JOURNEY.

Beautifully inked by

Beautifully inked by

Beautifully inked by

EVEN THE TREES GAZE IN AWE AT THE MOUNTAINS.

Beautifully inked by

Beautifully inked by

Beautifully inked by

BE CONTENT
WITH YOUR
INNER SELF.
BE TRUE.

Beautifully inked by

Beautifully inked by

TAKE SLOW DEEP BREATHS BEFORE YOU START YOUR DAY

Beautifully inked by

Beautifully inked by

THE SETTING SUN LEAVES A GENTLE PATH FOR YOU TO FOLLOW.

Beautifully inked by

Beautifully inked by

EVERY MORNING IS A FIRST MORNING.

Beautifully inked by

Beautifully inked by

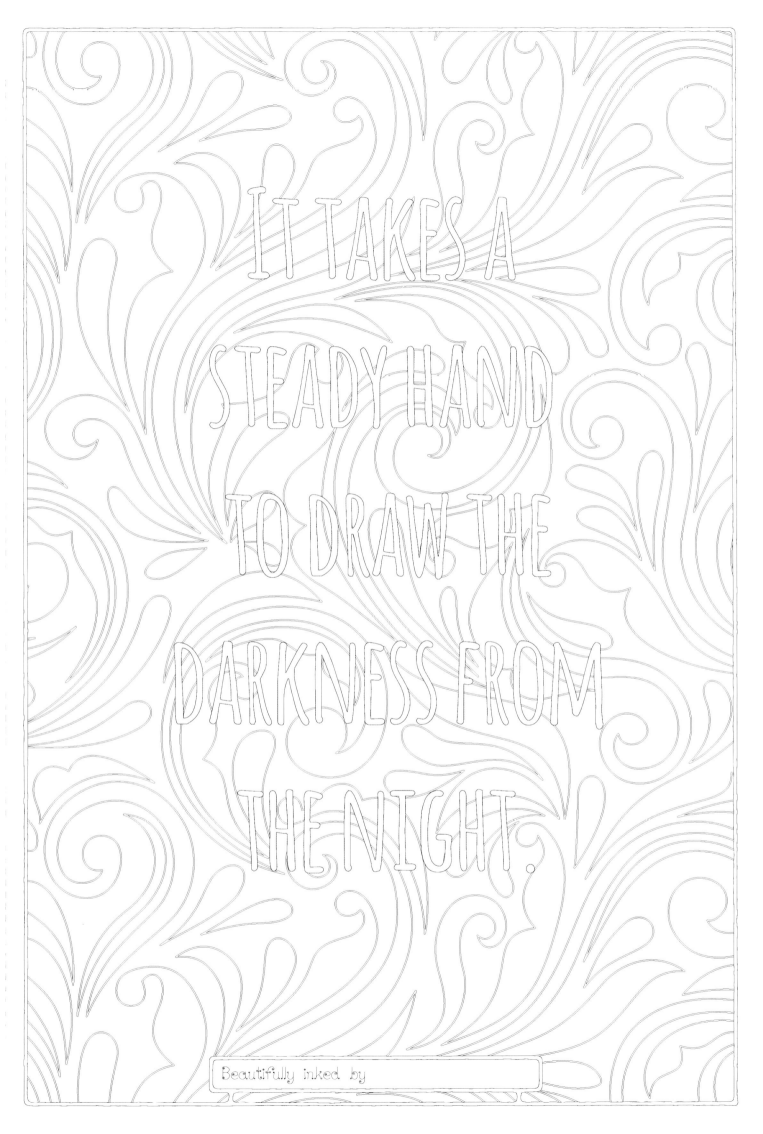

IT TAKES A STEADY HAND TO DRAW THE DARKNESS FROM THE NIGHT.

Beautifully inked by

Beautifully inked by

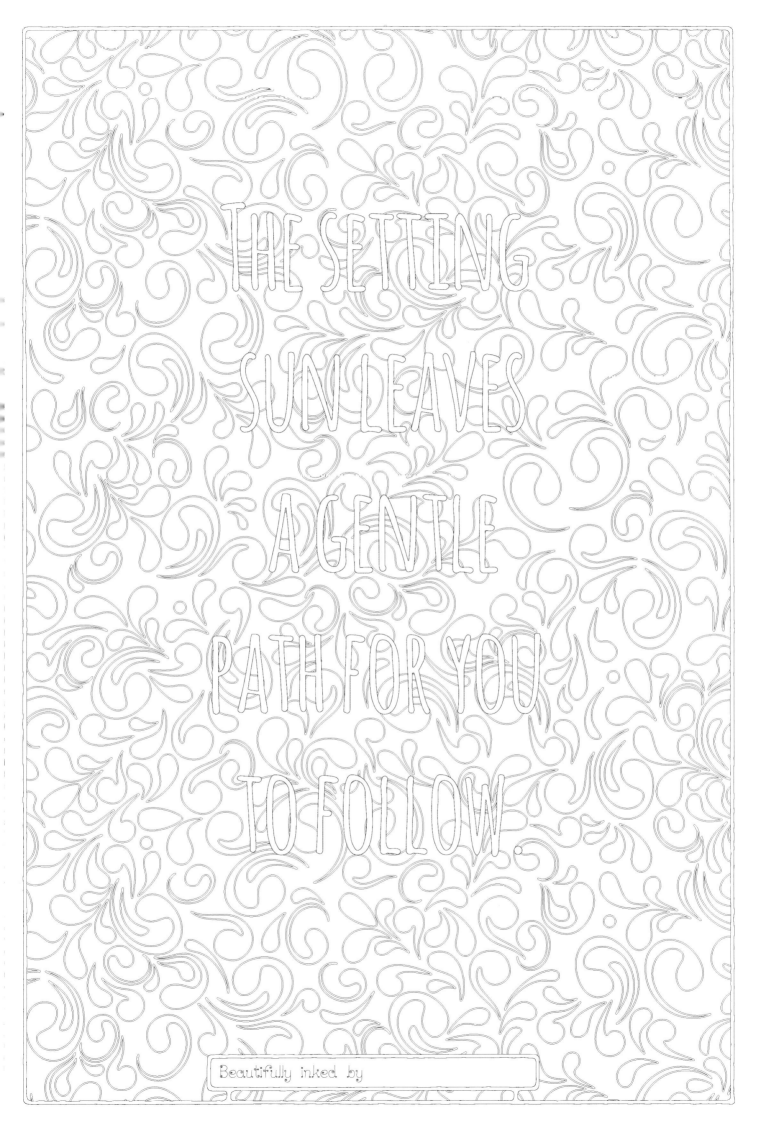

THE SETTING SUN LEAVES A GENTLE PATH FOR YOU TO FOLLOW.

Beautifully inked by

Beautifully inked by

Beautifully inked by

WE ALL NEED
FRIENDS PREPARED
TO REMEMBER US
WHEN WE ARE
OURSELVES.

Beautifully inked by

Beautifully inked by

Beautifully inked by

Beautifully inked by

Beautifully inked by

EVEN THE MOST NEGLECTED CORNERS OF YOUR LIFE CAN REVEAL A HIDDEN BEAUTY.

Beautifully inked by

Beautifully inked by

YOU ARE NOT WRONG TO BE DIFFERENT. YOU ARE NOT DIFFERENT IF YOU ARE WRONG.

Beautifully inked by

Beautifully inked by

Beautifully inked by

Beautifully inked by

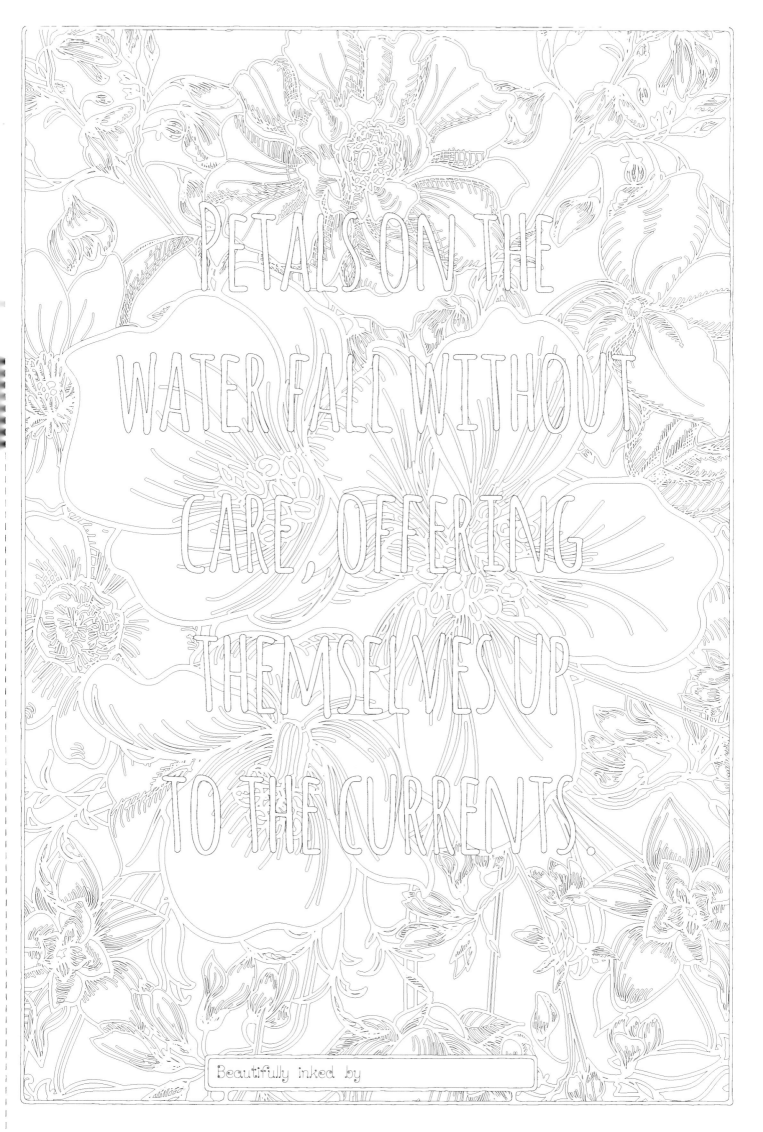

PETALS ON THE WATER FALL WITHOUT CARE, OFFERING THEMSELVES UP TO THE CURRENTS.

Beautifully inked by

Beautifully inked by

ON WAKING,
THE LIGHT INTRUDES
ON THE DARKNESS
AND SETS FLIGHT
TO ITS MISERIES.

Beautifully inked by

Beautifully inked by

Beautifully inked by

JUST TO STAND AND BREATHE THE STILL, COOL AIR CAN BE THE GREATEST TREASURE OF ALL.

Beautifully inked by

Beautifully inked by

WE SHARE DETERMINATION IN OUR STRENGTH, TOGETHER.

Beautifully inked by

Beautifully inked by

IMAGINE SILVER SPIRITS BENEATH THE SURFACE OF THE WATER, RISING AND FALLING WITH YOUR MOOD

Beautifully inked by

Beautifully inked by

SOME DAY WE WILL ALL JOIN WITH THE SEAS AND THE STARS.

Beautifully inked by

Beautifully inked by

SMALL STEPS, EVERY DAY OFFER, THE PROMISE OF REVIVAL

Beautifully inked by

Beautifully inked by

LITTLE POCKETS OF CALM CAN OVERCOME A LANDSCAPE OF ANXIETY

Beautifully inked by

Beautifully inked by

INNER BEAUTY COMES FROM GREAT STILLNESS.

Beautifully inked by

Beautifully inked by

LOOK BEYOND THE IMMEDIATE AND BE INSPIRED BY DISTANT HILLS

Beautifully inked by

Beautifully inked by

Beautifully inked by

FOCUS ON A DISTANT POINT AND ALLOW ALL THOUGHTS TO FALL AWAY.

Beautifully inked by

Beautifully inked by

Beautifully inked by

MEMORIES, LIKE FOOTPRINTS IN THE SNOW, TRAIL ACROSS YOUR MIND, SEEKING ANSWERS.

Beautifully inked by

Visual Arts

FLAME TREE PUBLISHING
flametreepublishing.com

From **How to Draw Manga** to **Tattoo Art**, **Alphonse Mucha** to **Drawing Basics**, we publish a range of fine and practical books, calendars and journals for artists and art enthusiasts.

If you enjoyed this book, please sign up for updates, information and offers on further titles on the visual arts at **flametreepublishing.com**